THE CELSIUS THERMOMETER

AN EARLY METRIC BOOK

THE CELSIUS THERMOMETER

by WILLIAM J. SHIMEK

pictures by George Overlie

Lerner Publications Company • Minneapolis

LIBRARY OF CONGRESS CATALOGING IN PUBLICATION DATA

Shimek, William J.
  The Celsius thermometer.

  (An Early Metric Book)
  SUMMARY: Explains the basic workings of the thermometer invented by Anders Celsius, which uses the 0-to-100
centigrade scale. Also discusses other thermometers.

  1. Thermometers and thermometry—Juvenile literature.
[1. Thermometers and thermometry. 2. Metric system] 1. Overlie, George, ill. II. Title.

QC271.4.S48 1975   535'.51   74-11898
ISBN 0-8225-0589-4

Published simultaneously in Canada by J. M.
Dent & Sons (Canada) Ltd., Don Mills, Ontario.

Manufactured in the United States of America.

International Standard Book Number: 0-8225-0589-4
Library of Congress Catalog Card Number: 74-11898

Second Printing 1976

How hot is a cup of boiling water?

How cold is an ice cube?

What is a good temperature

for swimming?

What is a good temperature

for skiing?

What is your body temperature
when you are well?

What is your temperature
when you have a fever?

To measure how hot or how cold use a THERMOMETER . . .

The word <u>thermometer</u> comes from two Greek words. <u>Therme</u> is the Greek word for "heat." <u>Metron</u> means "measure." So <u>thermometer</u> means "heat measure."

To measure **TEMPERATURE**
use a **THERMOMETER**

The thermometer that most people use is a very simple thing. It is a hollow glass tube about the same size as a drinking straw. This tube is closed at both ends. Inside the tube is a small amount of a special colored liquid. (Mercury or alcohol are the liquids usually used in thermometers.)

How does this kind of thermometer work?

The liquid inside the thermometer is changed by heat and cold. Heat makes the liquid BIGGER. Cold makes it SMALLER.

So . . .

The hotter the thermometer is, the more space the liquid takes up. The colder the thermometer is, the less space the liquid takes up.

We can tell what the temperature is by watching the liquid rise and fall in the thermometer.

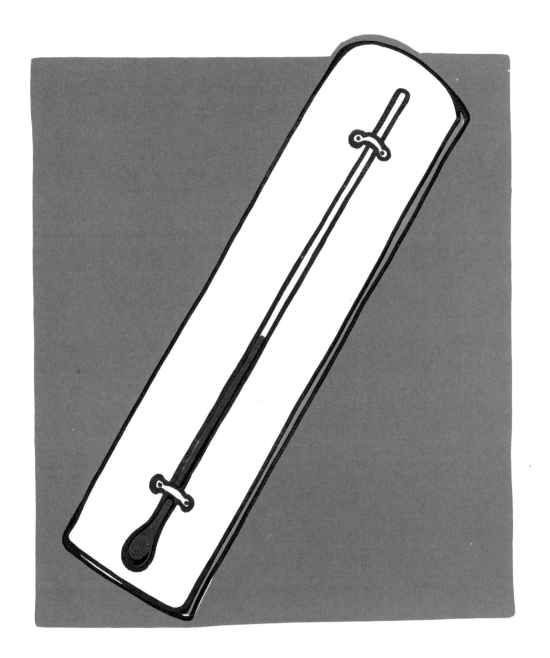

Many people have made thermometers. One kind of thermometer was made by a man named Anders Celsius.

Who was Anders Celsius?

Anders Celsius lived in the country of Sweden about 300 years ago. He was a very good scientist. The science that he liked best was <u>astronomy</u>—the study of the stars and the planets. After Anders Celsius finished college, he became a teacher of astronomy at a university in Sweden.

When Celsius was around 40 years old, he wrote a paper telling about a thermometer he had made. He read this paper to the members of the Swedish Academy of Science in 1742.

The thermometer that Anders Celsius made was named after him. It was called . . .

THE CELSIUS THERMOMETER

This is how Anders Celsius made his thermo-meter.

First, he put liquid in a glass tube. Then he placed the glass tube on a piece of ice. He watched the liquid in the tube fall, and he made a mark at its lowest point.

Celsius called this mark . . .

ZERO

Next, Celsius put the glass tube in a pan of boiling water. He made a mark at the liquid's highest point.

Celsius called this mark . . .

100

Then Anders Celsius divided the space between zero and 100 into 100 equal parts, or units.

He called each of these parts a DEGREE. All of the degrees together made up what is called a SCALE.

On the Celsius thermometer, the temperature of freezing water is zero degrees.

We write this . . .
0°

The temperature of boiling water is 100 degrees.

We write this . . .
100°

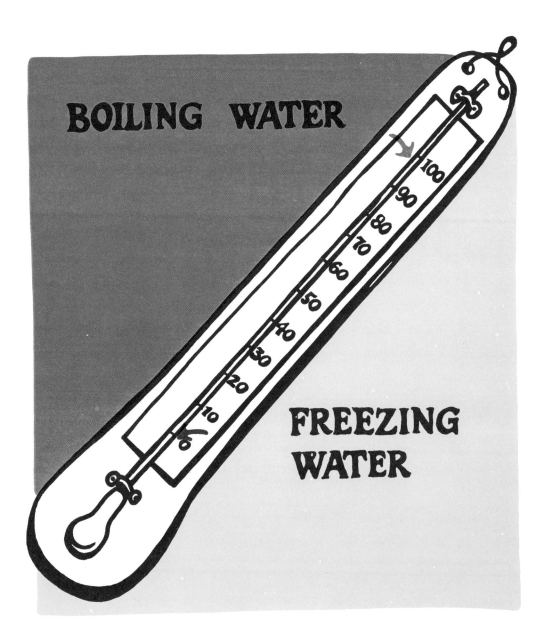

Each degree on the Celsius thermometer is $\frac{1}{100}$ of the distance between the temperature of freezing water and the temperature of boiling water.

Another way to write $\frac{1}{100}$ is . . . CENTI.

So we sometimes call the scale on the Celsius thermometer by a special name. We call it . . .

THE CENTIGRADE SCALE

By placing more degree marks above 100° on the Celsius thermometer, we can measure the temperature of things hotter than boiling water.

If more degree marks are placed below 0°, we can measure the temperature of things colder than ice.

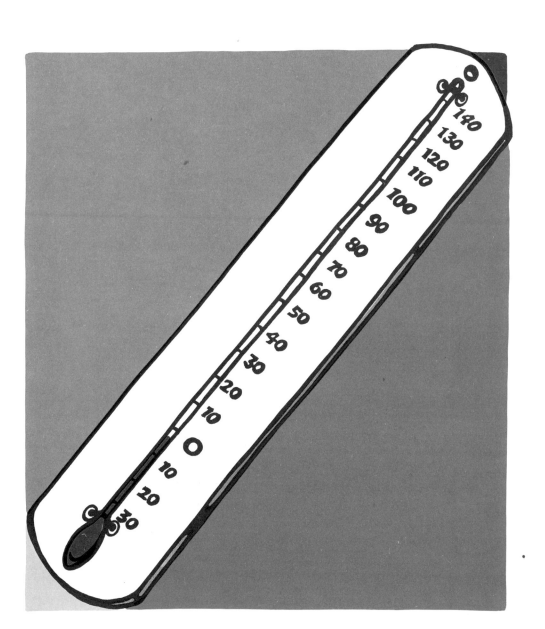

The Celsius thermometer can be used in many ways.

Sometimes we put a Celsius thermometer in our mouths to measure our body temperature.

If we are in good health, our temperature will be about 37°.

If our temperature is 38°, we have a little fever.

If our temperature is 39° or higher, it is a good idea to call a doctor.

When the temperature of the air outside is between 18° and 25°, it seems to be just right. It is not too hot and not too cold.

The temperature of the air in most homes is about 20°. The temperature of your classroom is about 20°.

If the temperature of the air outside is between 25° and 35°, it is a hot day. Many times during the summer, it gets this hot. This is a good temperature for swimming.

If the temperature of the air is between 10° and 18°, it is cool. Many times during the spring and the fall, it will be this cool. This is a good temperature for wearing a jacket or a sweater.

When the temperature is between 35° and 40°, it is a <u>very</u> hot day. A good thing to do when it is this hot is to sit in the shade.

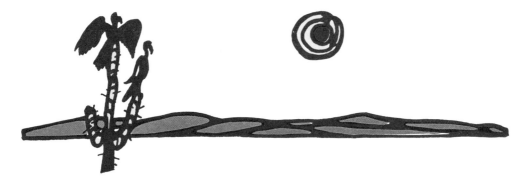

Sometimes the summer temperature in Death Valley, California, is 50°. People cannot live in a place when it gets this hot.

If you bake a cake, the oven temperature will be about 180°.

Set the oven at about 235° for pizza.

When we want to talk about temperatures colder than 0°, we use what we call <u>negative numbers</u>. Negative numbers look like this . . .

— 8° (negative eight degrees)
—15° (negative fifteen degrees)
—34° (negative thirty-four degrees)

We often read negative numbers in this way . . .

eight degrees below zero (−8°)
fifteen degrees below zero (−15°)
thirty-four degrees below zero (−34°)

When the temperature is between −7° and −18°, it is a good time for skating and skiing.

When the temperature is below −20°, many cars won't start. You might get frostbite in this temperature, so you should wear warm clothes.

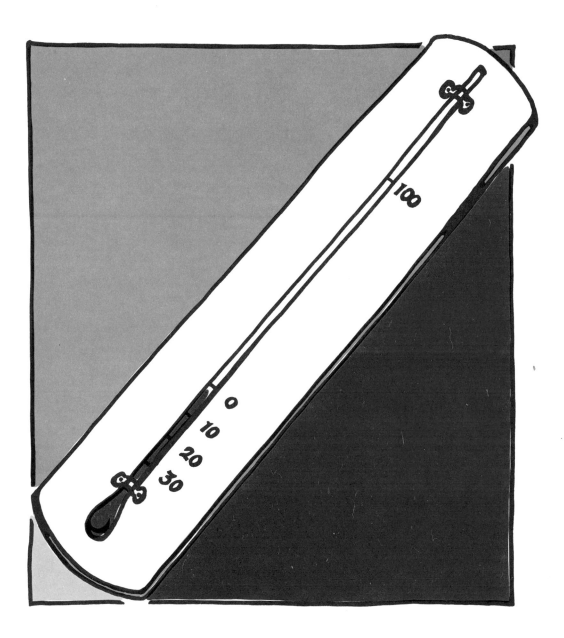

Sometimes the temperature drops to 50° below zero (−50°) in Alaska during the winter. When this happens, most people stay inside their houses.

Scientists sometimes work with things that have a temperature of −273°. This is just about as cold as anything can be. Scientists call this temperature

ABSOLUTE ZERO

There are other kinds of thermometers beside the Celsius thermometer.

In 1701, Sir Isaac Newton made a thermometer that had alcohol inside it. Newton used the temperature of freezing water as one end of the scale on his thermometer. The other end of the scale was the temperature of the human body.

On Newton's thermometer, water freezes at 0°, and the temperature of the body is 12°.

In 1704, Gabriel Daniel Fahrenheit made a thermometer that became very popular. Fahrenheit knew that ice and salt mixed together were much colder than ice alone. So he made 0° on his thermometer the temperature of this mixture. On the Fahrenheit thermometer, water freezes at 32° and boils at 212°.

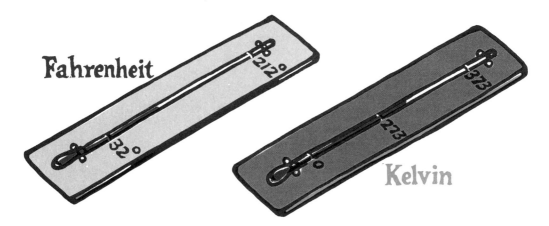

About 100 years ago, Lord Kelvin, a British scientist, made a thermometer that used the same kind of scale as the Celsius thermometer. But the units on this thermometer are called Kelvins instead of degrees. On the Kelvin thermometer, 0 Kelvins is absolute zero. Water freezes at 273 Kelvins and boils at 373 Kelvins.

Most people today use either the CELSIUS or the FAHRENHEIT or the KELVIN thermometer. This is how you can tell which thermometer is being used . . .

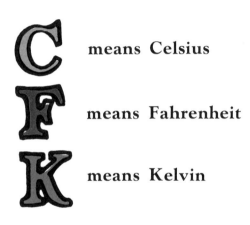

C means Celsius

F means Fahrenheit

K means Kelvin

The body temperature of a healthy person is about

37°C (37 degrees Celsius)
or
98°F (98 degrees Fahrenheit)
or
310 K (310 Kelvins)

You may have a Celsius thermometer and a Fahrenheit thermometer in your home or your classroom. But you probably don't have a Kelvin thermometer. Kelvin thermometers are usually found in a scientist's laboratory. Someday you may use a Kelvin thermometer when you study science in high school or college.